## PRAISE FOR THE BOOK

"A wonderful collection of poems weaved with a clean heart and a clear social conscience. *Staring Into My Soul* is to be savored and experienced in more than one sitting. It offers a mirror into each reader's own heart and soul. Brilliant!"
—CHRISTOPHER CHAPLIN, Honorary Consul; Former President, Consular Corps Association of Philadelphia; Inductee, Hall of Fame, St. George's College, Jamaica

"The language punches, the pigments vivid, the emotions raw... *Staring Into My Soul* delivers on every promise and lays my soul bare. Every inch of the Jamaican experience is explored in live and living color. As a screenwriter and filmmaker, I see the words flying from the page and transforming themselves into motion before my very eyes. From the tenement yard to politicians hustling; the remnants of grinding slave mills and the scorn of blackness to the pride of freedom and licking sixes; the ragga-ragga sound of a lead guitar to the silent prayer. I see it all so clearly. Rage, laughter, love, life coalescing into sacred pages adorned with the authenticity of the Jamaican tongue. What more could I have asked for? Take your time. Breathe deeply as you let the verses of a master wordsmith wash over you and invade your consciousness. Curtis Myrie – di book sweet. Yuh bad as yaws!"
—JUDITH FALLOON-REID, author of *The Silent Stones,* a historical novel, and *I Am No Poet,* a poetry collection; filmmaker, *The Gift Everlasting*

"Curtis Myrie's *Staring Into My Soul* blends intricate threads of poetry, harnessing the Jamaican language to create a vibrant and complex tapestry that mirrors the vibrancy of life in Kingston. Myrie's poetic reflections illuminate the resilience and courage essential for navigating life in Kingston, depicting the strength required to confront daily challenges and systemic injustices. He holds up for our eyes the sacrifices made for loved ones and the deep bonds that sustain them through difficult times. This work resonates with my own explorations in *Run to Freedom*, echoing themes of determination, courage, love, and sacrifice in the quest for self-empowerment. Three hundred years after the initial struggle against colonials, social injustices are wielded by different hands. Still, the thirst for freedom—sometimes smoldering, sometimes raging—continues to burn in the hearts of the island's people.
—DAWN FORRESTER PRICE, author of *Run to Freedom* and *Run to Freedom: Hinterland*

*Staring Into My Soul* by Curtis Myrie reflects his perspectives through clever verses, rhythms, and rhymes. His use of Jamaican Patwa revives the spirit of Miss Louise Bennett-Coverley, Jamaica's preeminent wordsmith, telling stories in a vibrant and poignant way. From humble beginnings, Curtis has become a successful spoken word artist and poet, well known in Jamaican poetry circles. His time at the prestigious St. George's College broadened his worldview, which shines through in his poetry. Drawing on his life experiences, Curtis explores a wide spectrum of themes, each timely and resonant, celebrating resilience, compassion, and the camaraderie that emerges from the shared human experiences. His poems highlight the determination and adaptability of people facing challenges, tapping into their inner strength to overcome adversity. *Staring Into My Soul* is a multifaceted collection where Curtis raises the bar with his profound

lyrics and thought-provoking insights."
—KWAME M. A. MCPHERSON, Commonwealth Short Story Prize Global 2023 Winner; Co-author of Amazon Best-seller *Heart of a Black Man*: *Inspiring Stories of Triumph and Resilience*; Ghostwriter and Book Mentor Strategist


"A prolific writer who masterfully weaves language, political history, philosophical truths, revolution, and the human soul into every word. This collection radiates a warrior spirit, delivering a powerful emotional resonance that lingers, stirring conversations and self-discovery in its readers. Like a silent river, its waves wash the shores of our consciousness with the force of a thousand waterfalls, inspiring us to embrace authenticity in thought and character. The poet's presence on stage mirrors the depth of this work. With unwavering confidence and a commanding voice, he draws the crowd into stillness, compelling them to listen. His delivery is both profound and magnetic, much like this collection. A highly recommended read for anyone seeking rhythm, truth, and the raw beauty of the spoken word."
—CHRISTINA A. V. WILLIAMS, author of *Pearls Among Stones*

## SUPPORT

Significant and generous support for this book has been provided by St. George's College Old Boys Association of Florida; Philip Wong, Founder of Deltana, an Architectural Hardware Manufacturer; and Attorneys-At-Law, Nunes, Scholefield, DeLeon & Company. To these individuals and organizations, I offer heartfelt thanks.

www.stgcobafl.com

www.deltana.net

www.nsdco.com

# STARING
# INTO MY SOUL

**CURTIS MYRIE**

*Staring Into My Soul*: Poetry Curtis Myrie -- 1st ed.

EBook ISBN: 979-8-9922741-1-0
Paperback ISBN: 979-8-9922741-0-3

Published by Gallery House Productions

*Consulting Editor: Dr. Vangella H. Buchanan*
*Cover art and illustrations by Phillip Taylor*
*Author photograph © Norman Thomas*

*Staring Into My Soul* is a book of poems and a work
of creative expression. Excerpts have been previously
published on social media and performed in public.

Publishing Partners:
Faith P. Nelson, www.faithpnelson.com
Andrene Bonner, www.andrenebonner.com

Printed in the United States of America

*This book is dedicated to the memory of Donovan Jackson – Jacko – STGC Class of '74 (November 4, 1957 – February 21, 2022), whose constant insistence and encouragement led to the publication of the collection. May his spirit keep soaring.*

*Photograph from the personal collection of Mrs. Ann Marie Jackson*

# FRIENDS

*For Donovan Jackson-Jacko-STGC Class of '74*

write it
in the soil of our fertile minds
*...friends*
write it
on the classroom seating plan
that showed the teacher
where we were
but never actually
who and how we were
students stirred
each class
each form
lids lifted off the boiling pots
of social ferment
marking mettle
how we were bent
voices raised
challenging concepts
precepts
but giving praise
groomed, guided
as critical thinkers
from boys to men
remaining always
*...friends*
fiercely defending one cause after another

with special notes to be made
of the mental rigor of *Jacko*
Donovan Jackson
pillar...as pupil of the graduating
St. George's College Class of '74
grand knight passing on
footprint that's imprint of one who's never leaving
write it
as we keep journeying
around each turn, each bend
leaving an indelible mark
as *friends*....

# FOREWORD

It is not often that one is afforded the privilege of writing the foreword to a book for which he has awaited publication for over forty years. Curtis Myrie had already produced a significant body of poetry which could have been the basis of a book forty years ago if only someone had sought to publish it. The opportunity to witness the publication of *Staring Into My Soul* is a testament to Myrie's boundless creativity and my personal longevity. Truthfully, I had no idea it would have taken this long for Curtis Myrie's poetic brilliance to manifest itself in a book. But as I hold this collection in my hands, I can say with complete confidence that it is well worth the wait. I am so happy I was able to hang around to see this day. For me, this moment is not just a singular honor—it is the fulfillment of a dream that I occasionally feared might never come to reality. This book represents the resilience of the creative spirit and Myrie's remarkable ability to distill a lifetime of observation, reflection, and expression into words which resonate deeply.

Although I am familiar with many of the poems included in this collection, I remain in awe of Myrie's rare gift for self-expression. His mastery of language and imagery continues to astound me, as does his ability to lay bare the human condition with such unflinching honesty and bold insight.

Curtis Myrie and I share a long and rich history. We grew up living across the road from each other on Asquith Street in the vibrant yet challenging neighborhood of Jones Town. Together, we attended the Jesuit-run St. George's College, where Curtis's talent and vision not only set him apart as a literary prodigy but also inspired me to pursue a career in the media. Even as a teenager, his poetic sensibility and ability to transform the ordinary into the extraordinary left an indelible mark on those fortunate enough to know him.

Curtis Myrie has always been a master of metaphor, a conjurer of imagery, and a deft navigator of the linguistic duality that defines our heritage. However, domestic obligations, and the pull of personal responsibilities delayed his poetic pursuits. In recent years, however, something extraordinary occurred. Curtis returned to his poetic calling with a vengeance. *Staring Into My Soul* is the delightful outcome of Myrie's renewed desire to express himself through poetry and to collate and publish his thoughts for posterity.

*Staring Into My Soul* is not merely a book; it is an invitation. It asks us to accompany Curtis as he casts his expansive gaze upon the intricate workings of the cosmos, viewing it through the mirror of his soul. This collection embraces a welter of concerns: the social, the political, the philosophical, but most of all, the human. Its range of emotion is vast; its measure of insight profound.

The very first poem, *Di Book,* in this collection is a cry from the heart. *Di Book* chronicles the displeasure of those close to Curtis who seemed frustrated at the failure of such a prolific bard to provide us with a compilation of his works. It was befuddling to many that a man so committed to his craft and so meticulous in his manner could have remained unpublished for so long. Curtis is deliberate, his words have always been chosen with care and delivered with a rhythm that reflects an innate understanding of the awesome power of language.

Myrie's poetry reflects an ability to see beneath the surface and to capture the unspoken truths at the heart of the human experience. Deeply introspective yet universally resonant, Myrie's work explores themes of love, loss, hope, and the eternal human search for meaning. These poems invite us to look inward, to stare into our own souls, as Curtis so fearlessly does.

One of the most remarkable qualities of Myrie's work is his ability to bridge the personal and the collective. While his poetry is often rooted in his own experiences, it transcends individual boundaries to reflect the shared struggles and triumphs of a community, a culture, and a people. Writing in a voice that is unmistakably Jamaican but clearly international in its accessibility Curtis crafts themes that resonate far beyond geographic and cultural borders.

As I read through this collection, I am struck anew by the beauty of Curtis's language, the depth of his insight, and the mastery of his craft. Each poem is a carefully honed gem, a testament to a life of contemplation and creative expression. Curtis Myrie is not just a poet—he is a storyteller, a chronicler of the human spirit, and a voice that will echo for generations to come.

It is a signal honor to introduce *Staring Into My Soul* to the world. This book is more than a collection of poetry; it is a journey into the heart and the mind of a man who has dedicated his life to capturing the beauty and complexity of human existence.

As you turn these pages, I encourage you to take your time. Savor each word, absorb each line, and allow yourself to be drawn into the thrall of Curtis's storytelling. His words will linger with you long after the final page has been turned.

Curtis, you have given the world a timeless treasure—a work that will find favor with generations yet unborn.

—CLYDE MCKENZIE, OD, M.A. is an international media and entertainment practitioner. He is an executive producer of the Grammy Award winning album Art and Life (Beenie Man) and is the founding general manager of Reggae Radio IRIE FM.

# Introduction

"Nation Language," a term coined by esteemed poet and scholar the late Edward Kamau Brathwaite, fittingly describes the voices of the many who populate the Caribbean. This language of resistance and rebellion is named variously (patois, creole, etc.) throughout the region. In Jamaica, this language of resistance called Patwa (Patois) emerged as a valid form in the dialect poetry of cultural custodian Louise "Miss Lou" Bennett-Coverley OM, OJ, MBE, and her call for embracing what once was a sub-verted form of expression reverberated as a form of subversion throughout the island. Musicians and other Jamaican artistes and poets heard the call and echoed its "rhythm and timbre,"[1] starting a revolution that pushed Patwa beyond being considered a dialect to the forefront as a language that speaks to and for the people.

According to Brathwaite, "the poetry, the culture itself" of nation language exists in "the tradition of the spoken word...based as much on sound as it is on song[2]." This spoken word tradition has its roots in the creative expression *Nommo*, a "characteristic of African orature," an African tradition that pays tribute to the

---

1. https://seai.web.uniroma1.it/sites/default/files/E.K.Brathwaite,%20NATION%20LANGUAGE.pdf

2. https://seai.web.uniroma1.it/sites/default/files/E.K.Brathwaite,%20NATION%20LANGUAGE.pdf

power of the word[3] and highlights the rawness and "irieness" of the "livity." The emergence of dub poetry in Jamaica in the 1970s is testament to the power of the spoken word with poets like the late Mikey Smith, Linton Kwesi Johnson, Jean 'Binta' Breeze, Oku Onuora, and Mutabaruka, among others. Along comes the voice of Jamaican poet Curtis Myrie to continue the legacy of the power of nation language as a force to contend with.

The poetry from the Caribbean has a unique voice. Its flavor is as varied as the smorgasbord of culinary delights each island offers. In this collection *Staring Into My Soul,* the richness and the uniqueness of the Jamaican Nation Language, "covering all the spaces where we fight for freedom," according to poet and author Curtis Myrie, contributes to that "one flavor" of the language of poetry. Born in an era rife with social and political upheavals, Myrie's voice evokes the spirit of the people who gossip across the fence but who are caught in political storms that are not of their creation.

Greatly influenced by Rastas who were "heavily into music and literature," Myrie speaks to and of the plight of the everyday man who must contend with politicians playing games and depriving the people of a solution despite having a vote. In his piece "Marking Dat X," Myrie laments: political halls/in a mess,/people's lives/under stress/yet you'll make the same vote again/blinkered.

In this collection, the poet pays tribute to nation language and the power of *Nommo.* The collection is at once a praise and an act of subversion. It echoes the "rhythm and timbre" of the language, resurrecting spirits and sounds long dormant. In Myrie's words, "Poetry is everything that we feel about what is resonating around us... Poetry is about the politics of the day."

---

3. Walker, F. R., & Kuykendall, V. (2005). Manifestations of Nommo in Def Poetry. *Journal of Black Studies,* 36(2), 229–247. https://doi-org.ccsu.idm.ocl c.org/10.1177/0021934704273148

From Garrison to Gordon House, the poetry in this volume is of and for the people speaking their own language.

VANGELLA H. BUCHANAN, Ed.D., M.A.
Author of historical novels, *The Master's Daughter* and *The Master's Wife*; Leader in Higher Education

# CONTENTS

## Dɪ Book

if mi fi follow
mi niece an mi well-tinkin-fren-dem
a time fi stop
tell di story piece-by-piece
go pass each mystery
an share di whole history;
doan post every minute
mek wi wonda bout yu limit
bind yu thoughts in a book
wen yu chat every-ting
weh come a yu lip
it may still nuh tek yu
any-weh pass di tip
keep di full manuscrip
den let it rip
stop mek it drip

but day by day
wi haffi talk
book write each time
same time wi speak wi mind

wen wi cry out
it's one chapta to the nex
wen wi bawl out
it's hot
an right off di press.

# GARRISON AND GORDON HOUSE

## ANYTING A ANYTING

story of bullets, blood and bangarang
anyting a anyting.
life means nothing.
born today—dead tomorrow
devil's dance, living with less
than a gambler's chance
baby pan di breast
chicks never nurtured in their nest
preying hawks before they hardly fly
hounds at our heels
nah tek no talk before dem hardly walk

heartless, senseless
left always lifeless
demented
murder, mayhem how we're branded
anyting a anyting
line that's character reference
story of our life's sentence

imprisoned in our open-air penitentiary
not guilty of any crime—but serving di time
in a maze—in a daze
politicians jus a gaze
wid a crime plan weh criminals ah grandstand
anyting a anyting
tings chronic—paradise in a panic.

## DI CRIME PLAN

me
a go dip mi mout
inna all di argument bout di crime plan
strait-up,
none a wi know
how it really tan
wi doan know a damn
cause wi erase and draw over every red line
wi mark in di san

stop recording
weh di speaky-spokey dem seh
dat a sham—pure scam.
snapshot stories weh neva tell how wi light di fuse
an to dem shock an dismay
to dis day
dem still no undastan di play

no credible crime plan
widout community policeman an woman
staying pan di groun
interacting, engaging
staying pan di corna
easing off trouble-mekka
officers
who mek shotta pause dem trigga finga
man an woman

those who yu transfer
seh dem too frenly
who largely mek wi hold it down
wen wi raise it up an spin it roun

plenty life dem save
community policing
truly for di brave
crime fighters
critically protecting
unnerved, unshaken
that is what you should be detecting
brute force cyaan be what you applying
if wi hope to leave our doors and windows wide open.

## KINGSTON 12

*To Marley*

shanty-shackling
tenement yard
dwellers
living in the street
red-hot rebels
in a rage
cyaan turn di page
fi mek ends meet
food neva nuff
tings juss tuff
dance up di lane
tellin yu plain
keepin yu sane
rocking
is Kingston 12
Rasta music
rub out di strain
reggae melody
that keeps you whole
Marley
soothes your soul.

## Inna Di Heat A It

inna di heat a it
meking di headline
every life
wi lose
a di news
beating di deadline
prime time
is crime
life sentence inna di inna city
shanty town penitentiary
everyday mi come a mi gate
a wonda
will i live fi pass di street corna?

inna di heat a it
an cyaan get weh from it
nuh so easy
fi jump pon a bus
an drive weh from it,
likkle weh mi earn
is a return ticket to it
an intervention haffi come
before law an orda
put dem foot pan it
anyting else
is beating
roun di bush wid it.

inna di heat a it
inna mi sleep or cross di street
mi can dead same way from it
doan haffi bi di target
stray shot
wi tek
anyone wid it
getting nowhere
widout wi all
tek serious stock a it
big talk fi park
nuttn good ever come a it
unda di gun
blood jus a run—
cyaan bline yu eye
nor turn yu back on it.

next on di news
could be
regrettably
how you were caught
inna di middle a it
right right inna di heat a it.

## Main Bout

yu a try
get ring-side seat
fi dis dub-plate political debate
top contenders
always have wi gainst di ropes
and even glancing blows
could floor our hopes

quite eager
draw yu draw closer
shutting out all analiss
dis main bout
no need nuh tenement-yard-tout

yu no waan nobaddy
a talk ova yu head
hard fi mek yu X
wen di ting complex—
all that's landing
haffi capture pan wi scorecard
shadow boxing
gwain stay right a yard

getting ready to rumble
technical knockout
if yu slip and stumble.

## Dis Yah Poem

difficult to pen
nuh care how much time
it tek yu roun di ben
start it in you mind
fi put it pan paper
you cannot write a line
hickory-dickory-dock
mouse get stuck
running up di clock
buzzing sound
before the blast
tick-tock...tick-tock

social load
haffi explode
persistent poverty
block every road
dis yah poem
you neva pu-dung
all wen you caan find yu speech
cyaan find yu tongue
tick-tock...tick-tock

poem weh stress yu
bad-wud fly
nuh care how yu try
fuse that keeps lighting

passions that keep mounting
rage pon cock
leaders never have it lock
buzz before the blast
tick-tock...tick-tock.

## MARKING DAT X

pimple weh tun boil
inna yu face
a spoil
each time
yu squeeze it
bump weh nah buss
wid all di power luss
fi di 3-card-man
yu bow down to fus

boil weh tek ova di whole a yu baddy
bruk out in a sore
every time yu march behind him more
fancy suit
dat neva hide
him still a brute
designa-clad
but him neva cute

political halls
in a mess
people's lives
under stress
yet you'll make the same vote again
blinkered
blinded
always misled.

# BERESFORD

*Remembering Coach and Teacher Joseph Sanguinetti*

he said
he wanted
in life, or death,
no damn-blasted poetry
man who always shunned
spotlight and headline story;
Joseph Beresford Sanguinetti
Joe...Sangui...names we all called him
Beresford
as I teased him

*Georgian*
Inner City
St. George's College
stalwart and custodian
man for school, community and country
coach, teacher
lifelong mentor
man in charge;
bustling, bruising
man slide-tackling
shortfalls—pitfalls
bellowing call
to avoid playing loose-balls

you could not shirk
he demanded work

*no double-6 pose*
dis no domino
get up an go
keep moving forward
towards your goal
all wen yu slip
trip
a reach fi di top an cyaan get a grip
he would hold you
quietly urge you
compassion
to gently persuade you

Beresford
*hush*—as he would instinctively bark
brave student still
would continue to talk
classroom chorus of street corner
larks
Beresford
please
*jus anadda word.*

## ONE TEAM

one team
is a dream
with any party scheme
unity
crushed
under heels
in a frenzied rush
for the best bucket deals

one team
in a yu head
share button broken
over the poor performance
on how you've led
quick fi fight out one-anada
chat yu a chat
bout working togedda,
blind-yu-blind yu eye to it
if yu really tink wi believe it.

one team
a pure poppy-show
taglines, labels
done-get-a-blow,
skin-teet an plastic smile pon u face
cyaan mask how political parties
tun cass-cass market place.

## OPEN AIR PENITENTIARY

most a wi community
a open air penitentiary
down-town or cross-country
hard fi find
bail or bounty.

jail time
cause yu poor, it's a crime
hardly win any appeal
basic pay
cyaan keep spinning fortune wheel.

life sentence
right up to remembrance
poverty a puppet show
pulling patrons on strings
wi keep jumping
an prancing
all wen politician
can only talk up di tings.

cell-block-tenement-yard
most remain
behind these bars.

## PR in ER

imagine
di gloom
public relations in emergency room
on its way to ICU
story dat yu spin
very political-round-robin
right back to where you must begin

whole ah unnu so bright
why common sense tek sudden flight
stop sell mi weh mi no feel
cyaan bait mi wid weh nuh real
so, package haffi strip an pull off
time fi stop tell story half-an-half
a nuh now dis a gwaan
long time conscience vote a pawn
slick an trash-an-ready
spik-an-span but still nuh steady
spin mi like gig
yu broad
yu big
but soul weh bald
cyaan hide wid wig
lie so much time
nursery nah nuh rhyme
an jackass still nuh sexy in a dark glass

cyaan cross
cyaan pass
spread out pon stretcha
nah stan up
nah stay up
nah add up
imagine
di gloom
public relations in emergency room.

## Yu A Shotta

yu a shotta
nuttn matta
who a get it
haffi tek it

yu a shotta
nuttn matta
who no scatta
haffi flatta
yu a shotta
yu wi fyah
even pan
yu famly memba

yu a shotta
a nuh nuttn
if wi dead by di dozen
yu a shotta
favorite hobby
is fi mek anada duppy

yu a shotta
jus a blaze
cause di dead
nah go raise
cries for you
fi mek a change

jus keep fallin
pan deaf ears
yu a shotta
nuttn matta
an di country
have no ansa

on wi knees
we beseech
even one
we may reach,
know tings ruffa
know tings tuffa
but how tings
a go get betta
jus fi keep on
pulling pan di trigga?

should wi all keep checking in
wid di undataka?
tell me, shotta
seriously?
dis is di remedy?

yu a shotta
all lives matta
aim at dat
and hold yu fyah
aim at dat
and hold yu fyah!

# THE NEXT WAR OF THE WORLD

the next war of the world
collectively
completely
is about what must be preserved
forget the bullies
men
boys
burly mannequins
may only temporarily block
what must be continued
makeshift-man-in-charge-models
must change
big man muscle
cause endless tussle
soup pot of scarce benefits boil over
cover never kotch right.

the next war of the world
is pounding-bomb-blasting
street-fight
supersonic missiles
never out wi light
men
women
moved
will stay in the streets
living, fighting, rebels never dyin.

muted
yet still screaming
through buttoned lips
at what's uprooted
we won't be acting as instructed
war will be waged
lives of the downtrodden
will be reconstructed.

# THE PALESTINIAN

I
am
Palestinian
homeless in my homeland
land of Jebusites, Canaanites
Ammonites, Hittites.
I
am
Israelite
land of Persians, Africans.
I
am
Ethiopian
Falasha–child of Solomon
and the Queen of Sheba.
I
am
Hebrew
steadfast Jew.

I
am
Palestinian
entire population of Gaza
slashing blade and stepping razor
majority population of the West Bank
overrun by settlers with armored tanks.

I am
Palestinian
Hebrew steadfast Jew
David's sling-stone
is my backbone
precision pebble against Goliath's might.
Marley's wail tells the entire tale
Jah-Jah children will stand and fight.

# The Resistance

the resistance
has always lasted
through recorded rounds of war
bombed but never blasted
missiles you keep exploding
men
driven
won't be retreating.

the resistance
while we're dying
has kept us living
you can't cut to tailor how we should fit
fabric of defiance that we stitch
is epic story of true grit.

the resistance
arm in arm
we keep surviving
against all that's detonating.

## Wi A Watch Unnu

tink truu wi nah talk
an nah really say nuttn
wi nah observe unnu?
wi a watch unnu.

fi get up off yu knee
nex man haffi pay di fee
while yu keep insisting
*it couldn't be me.*

pickney weh waan tek charge a di place
need fi know
it is never a sprint
a long distance race
woan mek no case
not knowing yu pace
it is more dan dashing to di mirror
to fix yu face.

such a rage to clear seniors off the stage
progress is engaging all age group
watch di peppa
yu a put inna di soup
careful weh yu serve
weh yu wish fah–yu might deserve.

interesting times
old bones like me
long time
stop reciting nursery rhymes.

## WHAT'S GOING ON?

when hit songs
become outcries
rhythms revolt
moods are makeshift melodies
questions are constant queries
Motown's mystic Marvin Gaye
soulfully searches for a pathway
beseeching
as he keeps wondering

"what's going on?"

cyaan know if yu numb
helpless playing dumb
sure yu see it
but yu blind yu eye to it
same suh, same way
dub poet Mikey Smith used to tell it.

"what's going on?"

beyond headline news
it is how wi cruise
while young hoods and hounds
light di fuse
pure led instead of bread
food a ration

price out a wi reach
but wi buy bleaching cream fi chase wi dream.

"what's going on?"

we're buckling
tumbling over and over
from all that's misleading
things tear apart
and all when *wi wheel an come again*
it is another false start.

what's really going on?

## When I Vote

when I vote
i remember always
why my parents and grandparents
placed their X
a baton passed
to my generation
to determine
the relay leg to be run
the same hopes shared.

when I vote however
it may not always be
the mark they made
conviction never prevents
a protesting word
against what we have always heard.

when I vote
issues that matter
will be considered
better not believe
dreams are traded
bought or even negotiated.

when I vote
mi naah tek no bait
poppy-show politician

no badda push mi gate
fistful of dollars
woan seal mi fate.

when
I
vote
3-card men
in whichever cabinet
will buss dem bet
days are done
when just a few go through
with most of us quite bereft
from fighting for scarcely what is left.

## WE WANT POWER

it's a story
i've shared
with politicians on the hustlings
story you could be sharing
with members of any political persuasion
story
therefore with no partisan paint
no brush to color any promotional tale
beyond the pale
story that's reel
of life's experiences
right before me
from my youth
the simple truth
leaving me mystified to this day
wondering if it really could have
happened that way.

this garrison marching group
was certainly no campaign troop
householders, housekeepers
mothers, aunts, and sisters
women with muscle
inna di midst a di struggle
who jus gyada
a dem gate
chatting as usual

bout weh squarely deh pan dem plate
how di worl no level
how it no straight
til dem start to buss a tune—

*wi nuh waan*
*nuh weeble flour*
*we waan power*

*wi nuh waan*
*nuh weeble flour*
*we waan power*

mi tek mi seat
pan di big tenement yard front veranda
as dem march up di street
no placard bearing protesters
no march on any media house
householders housekeepers aroused
clamoring for family dignity
children watching
hypnotized
the passion, the purpose
stirring audience
mesmerized
cry from the poor
from any party door
dem cyaan tek it no more.

*wi nuh waan*
*nuh weeble flour*
*we waan power.*

*wi nuh waan*
*nuh weeble flour*
*we waan power.*

## THE CALL FOR TRUCE

trying to stitch
open wounds wi a try hide
but everybody a si
call fi truce
could jus be a ruse
call so much time
wi no longer amused.

mind yu, man really waan
di hot-head war stop
men, women and children
everybody a drop
and after every senseless act of murder
sports day and dance keep
poppy-show pose
to get di people togeda.

if it never so serious
you'd laugh till yu weep
meaningful intervention a creep
community policing a sleep.

# RACE AND KULCHA

## Since We Are White

since
we are white
and it's really all that matters
barriers are removed
when we break and burn
at every turn
not being black
we are never driven back.

since
we are white
mobs are missionaries on the job
heretics with evangelical zeal
coarse, callous clan
every marching man.

since
we are white
we're covered with hoods
to hide our face
from this plain disgrace
deplorable, despicable
but described as even affable
selfies taken
supporters patting us on the back
beating, battering us
if we were ever black.

## SLAVE MILLS GRINDING STILL

*old slave mills,*
chants Damien Marley,
grinding slow, but grinding still
knee
planted on our necks
reflects
your perceived supremacy.

boots for more recruits
overstepping authority
call us thugs
when your toasting mugs
are our filled-up cans of gasolene.

babylon burns
at every racist turn.
it's not the fire
on the streets
you should be afraid of—
it's the leaping flames
spreading in our souls
flames that will keep burning
flames that we'll keep lighting
rage that will not rest
until there's change. we are not asking,
we are telling.
we're not our ancestors.

tek yu foot off wi neck
be4 di whole plate claat place get rek.

wi a go war
battles you can't win
because we're fighting from within
tek yu foot off a wi neck
to claat-claat.

civilization came down the Nile
you've placed our history in the wrong file
we won't be ruled
won't ever be loaded or pulled like mules
old slave mills
grinding slow
but grinding still
chained and choked
we'll never lose our will.

# STAINS

throughout the years
the stains remain
backra-massa's lifelong lash
tearing into our skin
scars, sores
you must keep dressing
wounds reopening
each vote
they keep suppressing.

# EMANCIPATION

emancipation
contract of abolition
served our imagination of being set free

increasing industrialization
ended plantation slavery—
chains removed from our feet
the results of projected returns
we could not meet

apprenticeship system
retaining us on the estate,
hemp-filled pipe dreams
on being allowed through the gate

emancipation
colonial downsizing
independence
more creative accounting

all shackles to be removed from our minds,
blindfolds to be tossed to enable us to see
what must be undertaken for us to be free.

## 9 Minutes 29 Seconds

one man
cuffed
facedown
neck
pinned
under the other's knee
pleading
gasping
increasing difficulty
breathing
9 minutes 29 seconds
suffocating
bound
strangled
even after no pulse is found
one man
lying lifeless
the other
completely heartless
murder
what else could it be?
eyes wide open
believe what you see.

# SEEING ME AS HUMAN

I am not asking you
to look at me
and see me
as a black man;
just open your eyes
and stare at me
and see me
as human.

# HIM BLACK EEH

*him black eeh*
childhood taunt
adult haunt,
black–an-ugly–like-sin
scathing tongue lash
across my mind
for the color of my skin
piercing wound
you try
to inflict within

*him black eeh*
*an him nose*
*so big;*
*good fi nuttn else*
*dan fi ben him back an dig*

pickney still pon di plantation
equality eludes every generation
even wen yu bleach
yu neva widin reach

*him black eeh*
Yesss
and you can't get it out of your skin
deep color of my dignity
keep splashing

against the pale canvas of your insecurity
framed portrait of hypocrisy

*him black eeh*
Proud-a-it
an it matta
all lives do
but have you ever
believed it's true?

# When The Lights Go Out

when the stage and stadium lights
go out
when the curtains are drawn
plugs are pulled
prolonged applause for our performance
no longer serves our cause

children of the cane-piece
to be shackled again in the dark
blackout
with each typo's whiteout
rights denied
race defied
rift
since we'll never fit the script
chokehold
defiantly we'll remove,
restive we'll remain
black and bold.

# PRICE FOR FREEDOM

there's a price
to pay for freedom
cost you often think about playing solitaire
especially when emotionally confined
shuffle di pack an pluck in yu mind
deal an serve
wat yu draw could hurt yu nerves.

freedom
price often beyond your reach
pocket change won't pay for free speech
pure political scheming and scamming
those elected are more conniving.

painful cost for freedom
but without paying everyday you'll never have it
keep protesting
out of your chairs and couches
up off your knees
price to be paid is never as you please.

## TIMMY

tim
is such
a tom
who ain't my uncle
memba dat
show window black boy
finely clad mannequin
you'd sling
on puppet drawn strings
poster pin-up
in political booths
vote catching, buying image
manipulating, disfiguring the truth
grand impression without conviction
sheer pose, posture of misplaced passion
a voice not his
coached, cultured
believe not a word
what he serves
is always fractured

tim
is such a tom
mere pawn
long before the curtains are drawn.

## THE BENEFITS

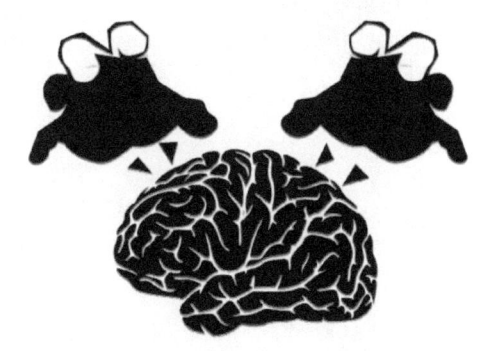

tarzan
weh di pygmies
leff a door
never have a clue
for what Africa
have in store
phantom
*ghost who walks*
dumb every time
whenever he talks
hickory-dickory-dock
colonizers with their bible
jus waan stop di clock
chain wi
but yu no certain yu tame wi
back again
with chapter and verse of barefaced chicanery
while scars remain of our torturous
murderous
transatlantic journey

sugar cane plantation production
true history shows
when profits declined through industrialization
you proclaimed emancipation
but apprenticeship
still lash di whip of designed enslavement

and independence
is continuing byproduct of colonial arrangement

you think
we've lost our purpose?
factory pool without the tools
so, we're not supposed to know our worth
and your benefits assigned
is only what you try to cultivate in our minds

tired ah dis
mr. desantis
tarzan
phantom
all that you illustrate
cartoon created benefits
to be left at your gate.

# THE IMMIGRANT'S PLACE

seating
at the head table
by special design
is how we're to be fitted
appearance that's often affected air
snapshot of being socially knitted
cordially invited
is the immigrant
guest who is no longer
anyone's guess
classy member of the colored team
whose right is to share
the *American dream.*

accepted at the table with good grace,
but family members hosting
politely acknowledging
are deeply rejecting
the immigrant's place.

## Keeping Your Tongue

we've not gone quiet,
button up
but wi really nuh shut up
frame by frame
smart phone pictures we take
digital slide
di rage in di streets of man gone wild
barrels of led
instead of bread
an yu tink wi silent?
garrisons remain belligerent

we've not gone quiet
man just mum
tight lip
watch yu back
wen yu tilt di ship
be aware
tongues keep recording
while wi tek wi time an creep
quiet rivers
always run deep.

## PLAYING WID MATCHES

child's play
striking matches
never imagined, all grown up
people could be playing with fire
parliament a promise
but ends won't meet
road, light, and water
ain't cookie jar treat
buckling
cause all leff is jingling
brains box battered
how every ting a go pay
cost of living rise every day

rage
will take center-stage
constant breaking news
angry mob refuse fi out di fuse
leaders looking away
match that's struck
is never child's play.

# REX

*Thoughts On Rex Nettleford*


Stature
that's Rex
man
mental muscle
child of the cane-piece
intellect—a complete continent

Image
that's Rex
man
a reflecting mirror
hide all you want
you'll still see yourself
black–-as you must be
black as you are

Voice
that's Rex
echo in your ear
sound
that's pulsating drumbeat you dance
to the creative rhythms of your being
motivating
stir soul and spirit
that's Rex
persuading us to rise

to shake
the shackles
of all that rattles
and retards
inside

Memory
that's Rex
black
bold
and free
his story
rewriting our history
color is no bar
defining the *smaddy* we are
we are set to achieve
what about us we believe
shanty town dwellings
never holding us back

Driven as Rex
there'll be nothing we lack
like the title of his essays
to guide and to teach
*inward stretch*
for greater *outward reach*.

# UNDA DI MANGO TREE

*Our Days At The Daily News*


unda di mango tree
rebels would rather be
writing at 58 Half Way Tree.

unda di mango tree
a di root
wi plant wi foot
nuh fraid fi tell di truth.

unda di mango tree
we climb
though wi slip
wi still grab and grip.

unda di mango tree
words fly
hot-off-the-press
learn how the voiceless cry.

unda di mango tree
wi light di fuse
passions blaze at di Daily News
challenging di state
change is never late
stepping back
neither option
nor our fate

rebels rage
yu betta turn di page
standing firm
any age
any stage.

unda di mango tree
we're free
highlighting the people's plight
all dem life is a fight
while the wealthy tek flight.

unda di mango tree
we share our views—
lead stories
making the breaking news
lead stories
making the breaking news.

# FAMILY AN YAAD

## SHE FIND WI TUNG FI WI

wi did lose it
shame fi even search fi it
prefer to be muted
rather than be rooted

backyard pickney
fi speaky-spokey
backra-massa blackboard story
no other way
to write nor speak
patwa was never meant
to reach this peak

gaze yu eye at this portrait of dignity
look steadily at Miss Lou
scholarship to the Royal Academy
drama that's revolutionary

she find wi tung fi wi,
tongue we're told
to hide roun house corner
caan put on good clothes an talk so.

so, communicating intelligently
is fi lose wi identity,
she tek wi to skule
fi set wi own rule

with tale and text to telling effect
first language is yu own
know what's adopted
to show you've grown.

pull di padlocks
from yu lips
from Sunday school to our sunset years
no lose yu tung,
lose yu fears.

she find wi tung fi wi
Miss Lou
tung fi talk
fi write wi true story
pon di blackboard of our own history.

# STRAIGHT TO THE TOP OF THE CLASS

straight
to the top of the class
straight
to the top of the class

what takes you straight
to the top of the class
what lights the spark
what makes the mark
what shifts your gear
from out ah park
straight from last
to the top of the class

straight
to the top of the class
straight
to the top of the class

time to move
get in the groove
pull up yu lace
each test yu face
shake up shake out
stop turning back
dunce-bat won't write
pon your bag-pack

straight
to the top of the class
straight
to the top of the class

right up step up
stop flipping up
fix up yuself
lan pon top shelf
find what it takes
draw up yu brakes
fast lane bring pain
what's there to gain

straight
to the top of the class
straight
to the top of the class

when yu slip
nuh lose yu grip
buckle up
for this roundtrip
no winning ticket
when yu quit

straight
to the top of the class
straight
to the top of the class

mek up yu mind
your strength you'll find
wheel up pull up
selector time
hit after hit
so get with it

top grade
top score
top class
for sure!

straight
to the top of the class
straight
to the top of the class.

## CLASSROOM EQUATION FI CONFLICT RESOLUTION

yu well waan
tek di stage
wid all weh a boil up inside yu
weh yu madda
yu faada
yu teacha
nuh understand
in-ah-dis-yah-race
wid di wickedest screw face
nobaddy naw tek yu space
nah tek nuh check
nah fail fi rail,
but yu haffi reconnect
despite di disconnect

values remain
through all the protest and the pain
and the poet
some always claim seh, *nuh know it*
deh yah fi show it

lock it
nuh badda cock it
all that strife
yu betta block it
watch yu tongue

wen yu waan lash it
voices must be heard
but du nuh dash it

equation fi conflict resolution
cause wen yu check it
it's never right
wen yu wreck it

mek wi talk
instead a bark
engage
instead a rage
have a meeting
put weh di beating
inside life's pepper pot
mek di reasoning
be di seasoning
listening
to each other
deserves to be preserved
come to class
bring bonds that last
classroom equation fi conflict resolution.

## Di Root A It

gig
spinning
head keeps turning
dizzy
inna di giddy house—
mighty Mickey is a mouse
eye dem spin wen yu draw di curtain
getting to di root a it
is only way yu certain

read between di lines
wen fake news fuel yu passion
you're driven by sheer distraction
digital platform
can spread pure harm
animals trapped
on di troll farm
all dat yu feel
more imagined dan real

analyze beyond di headlines
doan bline yu eye to wat yu si
dem waan tun wi head
to-di-back-a-wi

examine the gains
through grilled mental windowpanes

peel off the package
know what's in the kit
will neva mek yu giddy
getting to di root a it.

## Cyaan Badda

doesn't it
bother u
the least
the indifference mounted
when silence cannot be counted
each time
u should be raising alarm
about repeating harm

have u never
a fleeting moment
ever
looked into the mirror
right past the image u see
blinking at the shadows
at whom u should really be

after u fix
ur dress
ur shirt
ur hair
r u still proud of the selfie taken
full of life
but not yet awakened

r u just going by
hurrying by
right past the news
noting but not acknowledging the blues
center-stage act of being detached
despite stark images of the horrors attached

do u truly think u r really removed
unmolested by being unmoved
feel u r always protected
going in
locking u door
cause nuttn a go happen
claim you cyaan badda?

staying out of the way
might not prevent
u being overtaken any day.

## STORY COME TO BUMP

wat-eva card
yu trump
at times it ha fi dump
wedda yu a play
peta-pat or poker
sometimes yu haffi toss di joka
worth nothing holding on to it
betting your last on it
like di faith yu place
in di science man up di road
abra-ka-dabra
is quite a heavy load

stop believing every word you've heard
snake-oil-tongue swindler
sway every mesmerized follower
tik-tok-toe
neva-in-a-row
hold-him-Joe an-stop-let-him-go

wi know yu fraid
fi cut yu navel string from him
an no waan put in any-adda sim
blaming smaddy else wen it naw fit in
jus like him
wi ah katch an closely watch
di poppy-show

him ah huff an a puff
but can hardly blow
pop-style-poser
still the temper tantrum loser
story come to bump
dump yu han
larger-dan-life-leader
was jus a 3-card-man.

# IF YOU'RE WEST INDIAN

if you're West Indian
and your place
is in the pavilion
it's possible
each time the team tumbles
you feel the most pain
and not even the players know
how that hurts
losing what you thought you gained

as the *12th man*
on the hardboard seats
in the stands
we take the crease with the team
cringing as they keep collapsing
cuss pure claat
*man a wraat*

if you're West Indian
in the pavilion
a match
is not the same
as a game

our legacy is about tenacity
open the innings of your history
battle—neva buckle

keep digging in—
neva giving in
when you take the field
what you wield
are years of plantation defiance
cricket
is our rebellion at the wicket
each time yu show yu face
tek charge and dun di place

word from the pavilion
if you're West Indian.

## DADDY'S HIT SONGS

fathers
have their own catalogue of hit songs
tunes they keep playing
on the turntables of their souls
karaoke moments of moving melodies
hit songs
playlist
pressing through the pain all day long
rhapsody of rolling rhythms
for the family-man-one-man band
musical keys
often played with aching hearts and hands
trials endured
hit songs
for what's to be redeemed and restored.

# MISSING

my mind
in a maze
daily i am in a daze
ever since
mi little sister
gone
missing
it's been three years now
we still ask, *how?*
puzzled
perplexed
off to the corner shop,
how could she have disappeared?
now the worst is feared.

just 14
she was pretty
she was chic
kept refusing
to be the don-man's pick
in this zinc-fence jungle no one sees
no statement to be made
nothing to stick.

stories keep making the rounds
seized by men in a tinted car
speeding out of town

mi little sister
gone
missing
another likely victim of human trafficking.

security keeps investigating
same press release we're not believing
depressing
distressing
the days we keep counting.

# Happy Birthday Jodian: 4-28-2020

candle we light
cannot be placed
on any birthday cake
for Jordian Fearon
first time mom
dying, giving birth
just before her birthday
April 28, 2020
the public's pathology report of resulting panic
from the pandemic

candle we light
that cannot be blown out
each breath shortening

candle we light
heartache for crying sake
on this her very birthday
angel passing away

candle placed on every street corner of our souls
right across the country
flame that will not flicker
in any wind
leaping blaze of outcry
we let this child die
we live a lie

mask we wear
cannot cover
stigma and fear
right at the root of how throughout the pandemic
panic paralyses how we ought to care

candle we light
torch of protest
fire we blaze
against what's heartless

candle we light
defiant flame
burning throughout the land
happy birthday, Jodian.

## LOCKDOWN LOOMS

distance cyaan keep
in a di tenement yard
lockdown looms
an dem a draw card
so di virus spread
poor people haffi ponda
weh nex is dem daily bread
in a di crowded market street
in a di main town centre
bunch and bungle up so close
breeze can hardly enter
how yu a go get wi off a di street
wen wi haffi look food fi eat
an most cyaan stock up
wi nuh have di money pile up
rent cyaan pay
eviction notice pan di way
stress chip wi head
lock up in a wi house
is like strap wi in a wi bed
name tag caan deh pan di nex body bag
haffi exercise caution
but shutting wi down
still put wi life pan auction.

## Hold Yu Ears, Yute

hold yu ears, Yute.
all wen yu get tired fi ear it
try fi shut it out
but know yu haffi bear it
lessons to be learnt
wen yu hold yu ears
hot-head
never stop di tears
nuttn new
haste
may only save a few
acknowledge a place for us
continue to care
dat's a muss

life's baton change
will be a smooth exchange
reach timely collect it
practice the pass
in time you'll perfect it
engage
each step
each stage
there are customs to hold dear
unmute
hold yu ears, Yute.

## TEARS MY MOTHER CRIED

rock
we leaned on
root
we clung to
children
as family branches
while our dear father
tilled the soil
nurtured
watered
by streams of briny tears
my mother cried through moments
she needed to rinse her soul
never weak
crying tears of hope
to wash her cheeks
comforting us through our fears
assured embrace

mother's strength
always in place
crying
then with shoulders shrugging
spirit raising
rising
her soul now rinsed
backyard clothes line of courage

our lives laundered and hung out to dry
mother pinning
what's soak stained from all we cry
sunned by the rays of hope—
dear mother
keeps urging
my children
my family
we will always cope.

## JASMINE DEEN

still missing
over 100 days
missing from the production mill
of prime-time news
bizarre kidnapping case
story we can't get over
though we're not yet past the cover
Jasmine Deen
gone clean from most minds
hoarse
in our silence as sheep
screaming souls chokingly weep
*where is Jasmine Deen?*
cyaan stop search
cyaan close shop
brakes cyaan jus draw brap
*where is Jasmine Deen?*
finding her is necessary
by any means.

# The Timepiece

*For Pauline Stone Myrie*


ticking
like our very pulse
are the moments
highlighting the quality of our life
pages of our special passage
notebook
tucked under our pillows
that's journal of our days
refreshing stories
about bonding and endurance
chapters
we keep printing
of new beginnings
*happy anniversary, Pauline.*

## DI SELF AND DI SOUL

## FACING LIFE

you shy away
from the mirror,
saying all the time
yu a go face it
but shut yu eye
in front a it
each time yu stan up like yu tuff
pure powder puff
man weh blink
each time yu tink
yu can dress yuself inna new clothes,
covering up
how yu naked
facing all di blows.

## A Waah Write

muffled mind
struggling with expression
numbed—almost muted
a waan write
wings, folded
a waan fly
a soaring bird
darting through
half-cracked open doors.

# DANDY-SHANDY IN THE DARK

in the cell blocks of your mind
in your solitary confine
you play dandy-shandy with the dark
the children's game—ducking, dodging
what's swiftly tossed at you
by eager friends from both ends,
the same way
you slip and back away
from the blows the darkness throws

in the cell blocks of your mind
you'll have to trust your will
it's required skill
preventing you being pinned
from giving in

dandy-shandy,
same child's game you're still forced to play
swaying, swerving
to keep the darkness away.

## FEELING HUMAN

fear
makes us frail
tiger taken by the tail
souls on bended knees
beseeching the Almighty, *Please*—
lock pop off a yu Pandora's box
everyting fly an fling open
flat pan yu face
dare not beat yu chess an brace
quiet wail now replace di gale
a feeling not readily recognized
programed life no longer digitized
feeling human.

## FLICKING DI SWITCH

jus
flick di switch
an stare
at di images
on the walls of yu life
beaming close-up blurs
revealing
what you claim to be clouded

stunned
you stammer
you slur
so, you dash
to flick the switch in a flash
pictures to be deleted
captions to be cleared
right away
if you had a say.

## FLAT PAN YU BACKSIDE

sometime
yu haffi drop
flat pan yu backside
fi really appreciate
being on your feet
an it happen sometime,
to some a wi, an sometime
to all a wi

sometime
yu backside haffi bun yu
fire gash a yu tail
deep, deep inside
cyaan stop bawl an wail
loose and found wanting
falling, failing
efforts requiring
your redoubling

hit di retry button
a nuh nuttn
git up an try supm
nuh look back
nuh step back
nuh come back wid di same play
flat pan yu backside,
cause yu a stray

shake up
stretch deep inside
real measure of how far
you'll reach outside.

## GOD'S BREATH OF LIFE

Breathe
Your Breath of Life
Dear God,
on me
blow away doubts and fears
stir my mind
body and spirit
let me take those stairs

Breathe on me
Dear God of Life
give me strength
let me rise from off my knees
calm tempestuous seas

Breathe on me
Dear Prince of Peace
with that fresh and gentle breeze
bid my soul at ease
hold my hand
to follow Your plan
life's purpose now to clearly see

Breathe
Dear Lord
on me.

## Souls Saying Yes

*The Ordination of Edmond Johnson*

the Ordination
was their very own journey
candidates now as Chaplains
their souls
saying yes

months spiritually climbing mountains
bruised knuckles and knees
clutching, clinging
hanging, holding
bleeding, believing
their souls
saying yes

reaching peak and plateau
through inspirational pressures
weeping...wailing
tears streaming...soaking
the vests of their very faith
insisting, persisting
their souls
saying yes

the Chaplains' conviction
collar, crest of their very mission
chanting chorus of those called for Christ
spirits blessed

their souls
saying yes

congregation, witnessing
families, friends
all supporting
a gentle Voice
throughout the sanctification
keeps whispering
quietly urging
preaching from the pulpit within
say yes
through anguished fears
say yes
through cheek-stained tears
say yes
Christ always cares
say yes
The Lord never fails
say yes.

## LIKKLE DRUMMER BOY

pressing through the crowd
paying homage
to the Christ Child
here to see
Aunt Mary's
beaming Boy Child
at times there's a puzzled look
on Uncle Joseph
but no-baddy nuh watch nuh face
pure hush-hush
wi nah say much
jus waan go look
jus waan set eye pan The Saviour
weh three high priests
liberation theologians from di east
chat bout
creating quite a stir
bringing gold, frankincense and myrrh.

likkle drummer boy cyaan miss di occasion
kete-drum song melody
redemption rhapsody
reggae rocking riddim
marking the birth
of a real revolutionary.

## LIKKLE NUT TREE

soil
struggling to hold
what's to be deeply planted
root
needing to be nurtured

likkle nut tree
like the fearful child at kindergarten
timid, stuttering
but always shaping to grow
if even one nutmeg from what's still blooming
hope will be bearing.

## Movies Of My Mind

24 x 7 cinema
taking hard board box seats
to the movies of my mind
me alone
in a di full house
feature movie
wid plenty intermission
cause it is cliff hanging
story of sheer determination

frame by frame
pictures of *wheel an come again*
cyaan go up di straight
widout go roun di ben
draw brakes
but yu cyaan stop
buck yu toe
but yu cyaan drop

movies
wi buy a ticket every day
fi si wen pressure mount pon wi
main attraction
of what is filmed inside
me alone in a di full house
attentive audience
to the movies of my mind.

## PASTOR IN THE PEW

it's where he prayed
it's where he stayed
priest,
protagonist for the poor
the people's interest
first and foremost
on entering the church door.

Reverend Canon Ernle Gordon
pastor in the pew
placing the altar
in the aisle
the Christian's profile
priest,
whose passion
was the pew
where he stayed
where hopes for redemption
will never fade.

## PERSIST WITH ME

though You see
cast Your Eyes
*Dear Lord,*
at times away from me
in deep and in the dark
but still hold my hand
*Dear Lord,*
i plead
rolling rock
soul defrocked
but with life outstretched
i cry to Thee
*Dear Lord, Please*
i pray
persist with me.

## Staring Into My Soul

mi nuh waan look
a nuh every ting mi waan si
yet mi stare
compelled to sift through life
what's laid bare
rupturing make-belief
all not done from what we dare

mi nuh waan look
but a supm mi haffi si
soul struggling to find my place
in a crowded space
resisting the fit-in
what others frame
becoming wise to the rules of the game
my individual gifts lived
are never the same

searching now for who I truly am
my hungry eyes light up
leafing through soul's photo album
deeds and decisions captured
feelings and attitudes we still make
gently, I forgive my mistakes
heart grateful for my treasured keepsakes.

## REACHING DEEP WITHIN

yu haffi keep reaching
deep in your soul
wat-a-ting
all wen yu swet
wet
an tired
yu haffi keep reaching
yu haffi keep digging
beyond what's viral—
it's about what's vital.

in your soul you pay a constant toll
anyway di dice roll
cards dat yu shuffle
could still cause trouble
you are left bare
filled to capacity with all your fears
yu haffi keep reaching
deep within
reimagining
the new beginning.

# Risen

life renewed
from the ashes of yesterday
cross we have carried
hearts pierced,
nailed by our burdens
souls bleeding
the Lord's Hands
healing
closing all wounds
hope, faith
in Christ—in Jah
cannot be buried
spirits resurrected.

our souls sing
hymns of worship and praise
cries of crowding deniers
stretching to touch His Robes
we need nothing more
than to strengthen
our weakened will
risen
our voices will ring
boldly we meet
what tomorrow will bring.

## STARTING OVER

story for most
on all that's challenging
all that's tumbling
since COVID-19
story for most
on starting over
getting up
pulling yourself up
from the emotional couch
your spirit keeps rolling in.

story about getting up off the ground
from what's holding,
locking you down.
yu haffi tan up
shake up an fix up yuself
reach for your dreams
rise
ready to ride
propelled by how you are stirred inside.

## Salute to Excellence

it's never
a half measure,
excellence pursued, prolonged
is all that's daily to be treasured
it transforms,
we are never quite the same
defying the limits
we had marked in the sand
*it wasn't me* - we keep insisting
*no such line was drawn by my hand*
tiny steps we were willing to take
are giant leaps we are now determined to make
most of us protested just when we started
so much to do
how could we ever get through?
after the doubting
fears that keep mounting
there is that quiet voice in our ear
persistently urging,
*the excellence you seek*
*is always within you.*
lessons
we as students may teach
excellence is always within our reach.

# COMING HOME TO ME

waiting
patiently
on the prodigal's doorsteps
me
coming home to me—
left home
leaving
tactical bag of tools
kit left behind
with prodigious book of rules—
me
welcoming me
new tomorrow
to find today's pathway
that only my spirit may see.

# A Note On Language

The majority of the pieces here feature a creative hybrid of standard English and the Jamaican nonstandard dialect, creole or Patwa. There are two major movements of the ongoing attempt to capture what is now being called Jamaica Nation Language. The first is the more formalized, phonetic-based version, preferred by purists attempting to codify the language removing a host of variant spellings. The other form normally appears with familiar, English-derived orthography, accompanied by, or infused with, creole intonation and attitude. This anthology uses the latter, focusing on consistency and accessibility.

# ACKNOWLEDGEMENTS

I would like to express my heartiest appreciation and gratitude for the encouragement given by friends who are no longer with us – Joe Sanguinetti, teacher and coach at my high school, St. George's College, and my 1974 graduation classmate, attorney at law, Donovan 'Jacko' Jackson.

They would not let up.

Sanguinetti teased that the pieces written, like the farm produce cocoa, needed a basket. 'Jacko', in constant text messages, kept urging to 'put them all together and just write the damn book.'

Gratitude must also be expressed for the sponsorship provided by Jackson's law firm Nunes, Scholefield, DeLeon & Co, 1957 (the very year I was born) St. George's College graduate Philip Wong and the South Florida St. George's College Old Boys Chapter. The never ageing St. George's College Old Boy Dennis Barnett has remained a pillar of support. Thanks to Ann Marie Jackson, the widow of Donovan Jackson and to Donovan's law partner, Lowell Morgan for their support.

I must say thanks to schoolmate and lifelong friend Clyde McKenzie, who has written the foreword with special mention to be made as well of my late schoolmate and friend Anthony 'Zoanie' Smith whose life impacted what has been penned.

All that stirred has also been steered by my family. Thanks to my parents Gwendolyn and Alexander Myrie for giving me roots and wings and for their sacrifices which made this journey possible. Thanks to my wife Pauline Stone for creating space and for being the first to read many of the pieces early morning. She would smile, teasingly asking, "are you okay now?"

Thanks to consulting editor, Dr. Vangella H. Buchanan for providing the introduction and to Dr. Ezra Engling, independent language consultant, for striking a balance between the recognized variants that people our Jamaica Nation Language.

I am grateful to the Honorary Consul Christopher Chaplin, Judith Falloon-Reid, Dawn Forrester Price, Kwame McPherson, and Christina A. V. Williams for their generous and thoughtful reviews of this book.

Thanks to the team of Andrene Bonner and Faith Nelson for being publishing partners, guiding this book through every stage of its journey—from initial edits to preparing the manuscript for publication. Your expertise in editing, design, and project coordination has been invaluable in bringing this collection to life.

## About The Author

Born in Jamaica when political independence was on the horizon and the poetry of Claude McKay, Dr. Louise Bennett-Coverley, and Derek Walcott were a clarion call, Myrie fell in love with writing. At the age of 16, teacher Joe Kijanski planted the journalism seed, inviting Myrie and his friends Clyde McKenzie, Dennis Lyn, Donovan Green and others, to revive the school newspaper *Blue and White* and become its editorial team. National newspapers soon followed. Under the mentorship of leading journalists Raymond Sharpe and Tony Becca, his career took wings, eventually making him a mainstay in print, radio and television. Myrie won a Caribbean Broadcasting Merit Award for Excellence for his documentary on Jamaica's 1998 Reggae Boyz World Cup football campaign to France. A successful consumer marketer, he has produced numerous campaigns for the public and private sectors. Poetry remains his constant. He is currently performing with the *Jamaica Poets Nomadic College and School Tour*. Connect with Curtis at www.curtismyrie.com or follow him on Facebook to stay updated on his latest works and insights.

## Excerpt from a conversation with Curtis Myrie

# Livity & The Poetics of the Soul

Curious about Curtis' inner world and the circumstances that inform his poetry, we agreed to sit down and have a conversation about his new book, *Staring Into My Soul*, a collection of poems reflecting his thoughts on various social issues and life experiences. This excerpt has been edited for clarity and brevity.

—ANDRENE BONNER, Author and Praise Poet

**AB: How did life start for you? Where were you born? Tell me a little bit about family.**

CM: My family lived on Percy Street in Hannah Town, West Kingston, when I was born. That has stuck in my memory as all my mother had to do, when I was just about ready to come into this world, was to walk across the street to the Jubilee Hospital because of where we lived. That's how close we were, some 40-50 yards away from the Jubilee Hospital.

I remember vividly those early years - and then we moved when I was about age 6. You know how it is, the journey of the inner-city family, right? So, we moved from there to Fletcher's Land for a little while, and then we moved to Jones Town. I can remember, I think, at age 7, living on Asquith Street—16 Asquith Street. Those were all exciting years...the years of my youth when the Inner City was not the dark image so easily presented and thrown against the wall of our imaginings. The Inner City was quite colorful and full of life at that time, and I spent from year 7, I think, to about year 16-17 with all my friends. It was a grand village.

**AB: Tell me about your parents and siblings. I love that kind of story.**

CM: The rebel that we all became had nothing to do with our parents. In fact, I believe we rebelled against strictures because I had parents, mother, and father, who had an eye for, shall we say, discipline. Mind you, there was a certain tolerance for us being youthful. They gave you some space.

But from very early, you realized that in your changing world, you had to be marking time with a value system that was handed down to them and which should be handed to you.

**AB: Who would you say of your parents was the disciplinarian?**

CM: First, Mama...and thereafter you don't want more than one beating from my father for the year.

**AB: What were your early school days like and how did they shape you?**

CM: There was a church school at the top of Church Street going into Fletcher's Land with Sister Lou, the disciplinarian as founder and principal. From very early 5, 6, I can remember her using things around you to enhance the lesson she was trying to impart. So, from very early on you were aware of cultural things. And then I went to St. Aloysius Boys' School.

Aloysius is a Roman Catholic School. They were primary schools that were like high schools. So, the transition from primary school to high school was fluid, and by the time we were in

4th Grade, though still too young, we were quite ready for high school because the teaching was good.

**AB: What role did poetry and literature play in your life growing up? Did you find yourself memorizing poetry in those early days?**

CM: You were encouraged to do your schoolwork but to participate in all types of things. Outside of running up and down in the schoolyard, there was music, and there was drama. I took part in various concerts. I was a member of the festival gold medal choir of St. Aloysius.

Around 1969 and in the seventies, while in high school, you were consumed by the culture – and quite conscious about Rasta.

Clyde McKenzie, former Head Boy of St. George's, grew up on the same Asquith Street. And by the way, Asquith Street would produce more than one Head Boy because my younger brother Kirk also became a Head Boy. I remember the Dean of Discipline, Father Quinlan joking that the votes had gone left. He was using a geographic and political pun to describe the Head Boy phenomenon. We grew up on Asquith Street beside Rastafarians who were heavily into music and literature. These were very cerebral men. I was having lunch with classmates the other day, and I was telling them that at age 13-14, Clyde and I would regularly go next door to Samah Reid (Gussie), who was like a reserve member of the Mystic Revelation of Rastafari.

During summertime we would be in the audience watching Gussie and friends who were fantastic musicians. They played various genres of music—from Afrocentric beats and rhythms to jazz and even scores from the Sound of Music. So, this thing about the Inner City just being a particular way of life is nonsense! The sixties, coming into the seventies, even when things boiled during the mid-seventies to the eighties, the Inner City was still a stirring melting pot of cultures and a vehicle for all sorts of expressions and impressions impacting your daily life.

**AB: It was quite rich. How does your family inspire and support you in your creative writing and other writing endeavors?**

CM: The family allowed everybody to be everybody. You just were allowed to do your thing. My brother, Kirk, was like my father, multi skilled. We all played sports and were also involved in academic games—various school quizzes in your own backyard. I just naturally liked to write. I started writing poetry from about 3rd or 4th form at George's.

**AB: What is the creative climate in your household now?**

CM: I'm married over 40 years to Pauline Stone, talented actress and shared a household for many years with stepson and my own children. Melting pot each day you keep the lid on (laugh)—made easier because no one gets in the other's way...with everyone's personal growth largely allowed.

**AB: I know that you've had a very storied life as a journalist. What kinds of stories did you cover?**

CM: All sorts of stories were covered - from what was daily assigned as an accredited sports reporter to my own initiative writing news, special features and creating my own sports programs for radio and television. I owe everything to a man by the name of Joe Kijanski, a Polish American who came to St. George's College. He came to class every day encouraging discussions about social topics that were of particular interest to us, ensuring increasing ease with English Language as a subject to be engaged. So, you were comfortable then speaking the language, just as you were comfortable using the vernacular, because you were presenting and defending various premises in a structured way. You learnt to argue, you learnt to be comfortable in yourself, with yourself, without being insecure about what was coming from within.

**AB: I see that your poetry is a mix of English and Patwa, the vernacular as you have expressed it.**

CM: Yes, it is—a blending model—at any given time to write and speak and there's no discomfort to do that. Absolutely none.

**AB: And then there is a generation that had the Honorable Dr. Louise Bennett Coverley, who also wrote in both languages.**

CM: We tend to forget that this lady was awarded a scholarship to the Royal Academy of Arts in the UK. Yeah. So, if anyone knew how to 'speaky-spokey' it was Miss Lou. Her cultural expressions in our own tongue was therefore a matter of choice.

**AB: Let's get back to Mr. Kijanski, your English teacher.**

CM: He restarted the *Blue and White Newspaper* at St. George's College. Clyde McKenzie, Dennis Lyn, the late Anthony Smith, Donovan 'Bunny' Green, Anthony East and I—that was the team. Everything around us was being addressed and that started in 4th Form. Mr. Kijanski then came to me, Clyde and Bunny and said, "Listen! The sports editor of the *Gleaner*, Raymond Sharp (deceased), got a copy of the *Blue and White*, and he's interested in getting a number of you guys to do holiday jobs as freelancers. Are you interested?" That's how it started.

**AB: What about the *Daily News*?**

CM: I left 6th Form and went to the Daily News. First, I tried to get work in the financial sector, but there were no vacancies. So reluctantly, I returned to my roots. The late Tony Becca, Sports Editor said, simply said, *You're not green because you have been doing this from 4th Form. Come on board. A job is here for you.* The Jamaica Daily News was a fascinating cradle not just for our literary skills, but for critical thinking as the likes of Terry Smith, Canute James, Hubert Gray, Carl Wint, Thorald deMercado, Leslie Miles and others challenged you to be developing different angles to stories.

You were encouraged to write everything. You were also encouraged to go down to the photographic department, and Mr. Charles Kinkead would give you a big box camera so that you could go on the street to become a photojournalist. You could quarrel all you want. You were going to do it. You were also taught to subedit, to plan a page. Oh, how I hated it! After all your protestations you realized how complete a person you were becoming that served other skill sets later acquired in radio and television production and even in marketing.

**AB: How long did it take you to write, *Staring Into My Soul*?**

CM: It's a collection of poems over years – answering first the call of late teacher and coach Joe Sanguinetti who kept teasing about doing *one-one and never a basket*. Then finally addressing the urgings—and at times reprimands—of classmate, the late Donovan Jackson, attorney at law.

He would come across my poems from time to time and would immediately send texts about producing a book. *Lord, I like it*, the text would sometimes read, *but you just all over the damn place. You can't write a book?* May his spirit keep soaring.

**AB: I can see why the book is dedicated to him. Now, I want to talk to you about themes that run through your work—injustice, inequality, vestiges of slavery on a post-colonial society. How did they make their way into your writing?**

CM: My writing is about conversations within, hence the title, and these themes are largely about what's striking in my life's experience. You see, poetry is everything that resonates around us—and each feeling is about your very fiber and all that makes you up. Uniquely it reflects what your social DNA expresses.

**AB: That is powerful. Is there another book?**

CM: Yes. I'll just keep them all quietly together, and when I'm ready, I'll just bawl, call yu and say, see it yah (laugh).

**AB: As we say in showbiz: To be continued.**

www.ingramcontent.com/pod-product-compliance
Lightning Source LLC
Chambersburg PA
CBHW021204130626
46554CB00005B/1974